Month-by-Month
Math Practice Pages

★ ☉ ★ ⊙ ★ ⊙ ★ ☉ ★ ⊙ ★

by Mary Rosenberg

NEW YORK • TORONTO • LONDON • AUCKLAND • SYDNEY

MEXICO CITY • NEW DELHI • HONG KONG • BUENOS AIRES

Teaching *Resources*

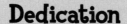

Dedication

To my number one fans—
Mom and Dad.
Thank you for all of your love
and encouragement.

Cover design by James Sarfati

Cover and interior artwork by Maxie Chambliss

Interior design by Sydney Wright

ISBN: 0-439-45874-9
Copyright © 2004 by Mary Rosenberg

All rights reserved. Published by Scholastic Inc.
Printed in the U.S.A.

3 4 5 6 7 8 9 10   40   13 12 11 10 09 08 07 06 05 04

Contents

Introduction

Welcome to *Month-by-Month Math Practice Pages*! These fun and interactive math activities are designed to capture children's interest and build essential math skills all year long.

Each reproducible activity page complements the math subjects taught in school and serves as a handy springboard for practicing specific skills. The activities help students learn the important math skills addressed in the National Council of Teachers of Mathematics (NCTM) standards for first and second grade. (Refer to the skills matrix on page 9.) Math topics within those content and process standards include addition, subtraction, patterns, money, measurement, time, and graphing. Within each topic, math practice pages address similar skills and concepts using a variety of approaches, providing children with opportunities to learn according to their individual learning styles. What's more, students will love them!

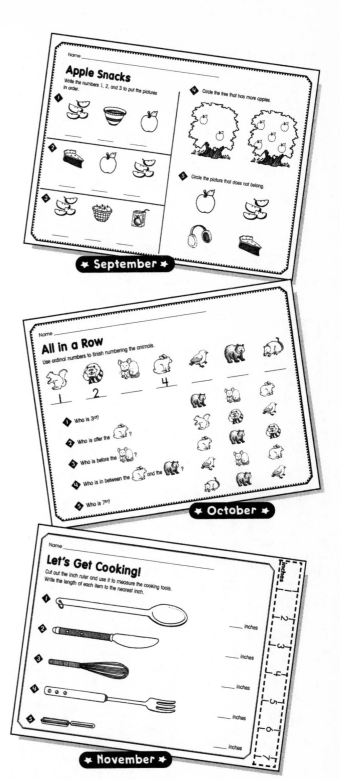

How to Use Math Practice Pages

Month-by-Month Math Practice Pages is designed so that it can be used in a variety of settings and situations. Simply photocopy the math practice pages you want to use, and you're ready to go!

Consider using the math practice pages in any or all of the following ways:

◯ **Preview and review:** Math practice pages may be used to introduce new concepts or skills to students and to review concepts already learned.

◯ **Learning center activities:** You can photocopy and assemble the pages into individual learning packets. For example, all of the pages about the concept of time can be assembled for children to use as individual learning center activities for a unit on time.

◯ **Quick checks:** Math practice pages may be used as diagnostic tools. They're a handy way to assess whether a child already knows a concept or is grasping a new concept. Students aren't likely to feel that they are being "tested" because the activities are both fun and engaging.

Homework: Families and children will find that math practice pages are straightforward to use and enhance school learning. Plus, each practice page gives kids lots of opportunities to show their family what they are learning, what they've mastered, and where they might need some extra guidance.

Helpful Hints

The following are some suggestions to make using math practice pages productive for both you and students:

★ The first few times that children use the math practice pages, show them how the page is set up. There are often pictures to cut out on the right-hand side of the pages. Help students to understand that they should have a pencil, a pair of scissors, crayons, and glue handy when they work with a math page. At times they may need paper clips and dice. If you are using the math practice pages in a learning center, keep those materials easily accessible for children.

★ In math practice pages with number boxes, show students beforehand how addition and subtraction can work within these boxes.

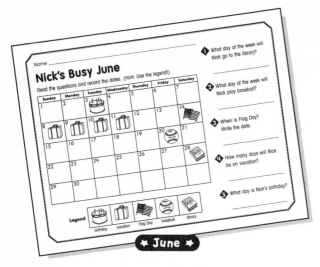

★ Encourage children to color the practice page after they've completed the activities on it.

★ Have students develop stories that show how numbers can be used in real or imaginative settings. For example, with "Back-to-School Patterns" (page 12), have children look around the room and develop patterns with the objects they see. A student may say "clock, desk, clock, desk" and then invite another child to complete and name the pattern: "Clock, desk. The pattern is ABABAB." The more students use words to help them understand numbers, the more fluent they will be in both expressive language and mathematics.

Connections With the NCTM Standards

The activity pages in *Month-by-Month Practice Pages* are linked with the NCTM's content and process standards on the first and second grade levels. For reference as you plan daily lessons, look at the skills matrix on page 9. There you'll find the primary skill, on which the math page focuses, drawn from the NCTM standards for content and processes: number and operations; patterns, functions, and algebra; geometry and spatial sense; measurement; data analysis, statistics, and probability; problem solving; reasoning; communication; connections; and representation.

Learn more about the NCTM standards by visiting the Web site:
www.nctm.org/standards/gradeband.htm

Connections With the NCTM Standards

Activity	Number and Operations	Patterns, Functions, and Algebra	Geometry and Spatial Sense	Measurement	Data Analysis, Statistics, and Probability	Problem Solving	Reasoning and Proof	Communication	Connections	Representation
SEPTEMBER										
Counting Apple Seeds	•									
Back-to-School Patterns		•								
Picking Apples	•	•								
Garden Shop	•					•				
Count the Crop!	•				•	•				
Apple Snacks	•									
A Day With Apples	•									
Apple Pie Pictures			•			•				
OCTOBER										
Create a Jack-o'-Lantern!	•					•				
On Halloween Night	•					•				
Scarecrow Numbers	•									
(Not So) Scary Characters!	•			•						
Spooky Symmetry			•							
What's in the Tree?	•				•	•				
All in a Row	•		•			•				
Tasty Treats	•									
NOVEMBER										
Find the Snack!	•		•							
Farm Clues	•		•							
Turkey Tally	•									•
November Numbers	•					•				
It Happens in November	•				•	•				
Color the Cornucopia!			•			•				
Let's Get Cooking!	•			•						
After the Harvest	•	•						•		
DECEMBER										
Candles and Coins	•									
The Colors of Kwanzaa	•					•				
Decorations Everywhere!	•				•	•				
Help the Reindeer!	•					•				
Festive Patterns		•								
Holiday Fractions	•		•							
Gift Boxes	•			•						
Gingerbread People	•				•	•				
JANUARY										
Winter Wear	•				•	•				
Making Hundreds	•					•				
Cold Weather Animals	•				•	•				
Martin Luther King, Jr.	•					•	•			
Name Patterns	•	•						•		
Counting by 10s	•	•								
Snowman Math	•									
Mittens on the Clothesline	•									
FEBRUARY										
Valentine Cards						•		•		
Sweethearts	•									
Three in a Line	•					•				
Fact Families	•	•				•				
With Minutes to Go!	•					•				
Our First President	•					•				
Our 16th President	•					•				
Dental Health Supplies	•									
MARCH										
Lively Leprechauns			•			•				
Pots of Gold	•									
Spot the Pattern!		•								•
Lucky Fractions		•	•							
Weather Report	•					•		•		
Colorful Kites	•									
Flower Petals	•	•								
Spring Happenings	•					•				
APRIL										
Fishing Season	•	•				•				
Bunny Math	•									
The Egg Mystery	•					•				
Mopsy's Garden	•		•			•				
More Than a Dozen	•		•			•				
Let's Recycle!	•					•			•	
Will It Happen Today?						•			•	
Give Me Five!	•	•								
MAY										
Making Bouquets	•									
It's Spring!	•					•				
Green Thumbs	•					•				
Sport Shop	•					•				
Memorial Day Parade	•					•			•	
In the Neighborhood			•			•				
Flower Care	•					•				
Plenty of Plants	•					•				
JUNE										
Tie Patterns		•								•
Nick's Busy June	•					•			•	
Safe and Sound	•					•			•	
Warm-Weather Weights	•			•						
How Tall?	•			•						
Snack Time	•					•				
Multiplication Riddles	•									
Riverbank Division	•									

Counting Apple Seeds

Count the seeds in each apple. Write the matching number word in the crossword puzzle. (Hint: Use the word bank!)

Word Bank

0 = zero	6 = six
1 = one	7 = seven
2 = two	8 = eight
3 = three	9 = nine
4 = four	10 = ten
5 = five	

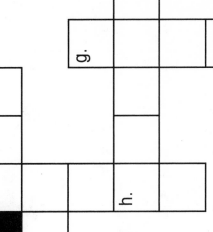

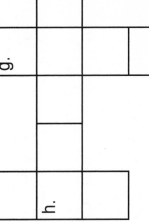

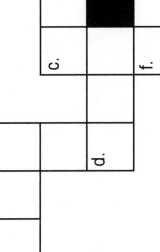

ACROSS

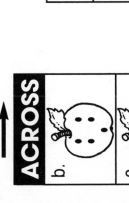

DOWN

11

Name _____

Back-to-School Patterns

Finish labeling each pattern.

1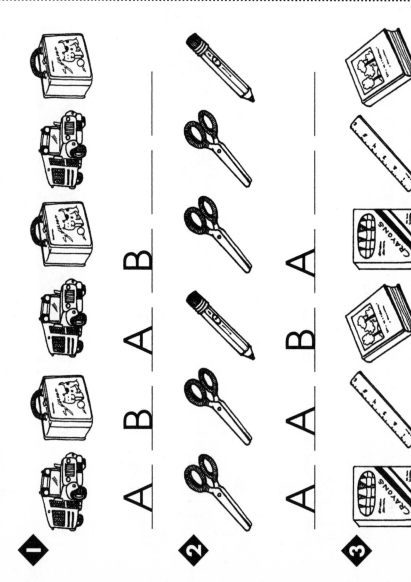

A B A

2

A A B A

3

A B C A

Look at each pattern. What kind of pattern is it? Circle the answer.

4

AAB   AB

5

ABC   ABB

6

ABC   ABBC

Use crayons to color an ABB pattern.

7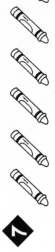

Month-by-Month Math Practice Pages Scholastic Teaching Resources

Name _____

Picking Apples

How many apples are on the tree? How many are below the tree?
Count each group of apples. Then write and solve the addition problem.

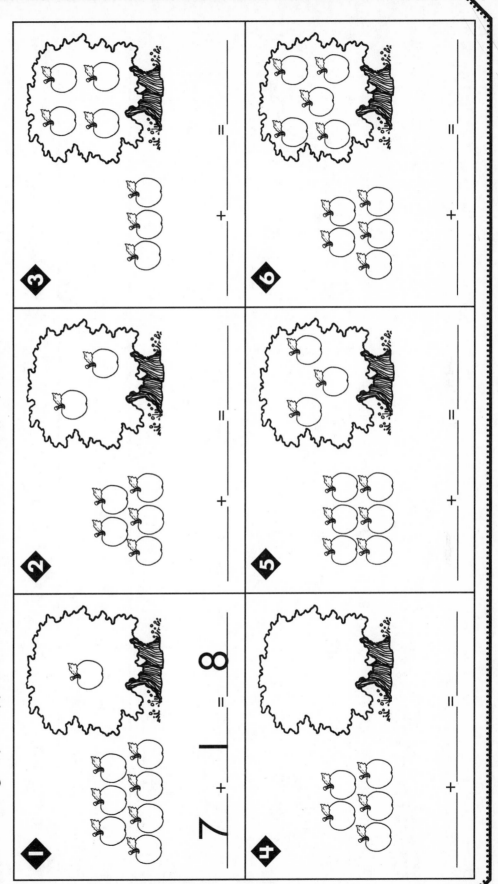

1

$$7 + 1 = 8$$

2

___ + ___ = ___

3

___ + ___ = ___

4

___ + ___ = ___

5

___ + ___ = ___

6

___ + ___ = ___

Name _____

Garden Shop

Count the pennies you need to buy each garden item. Write the price.

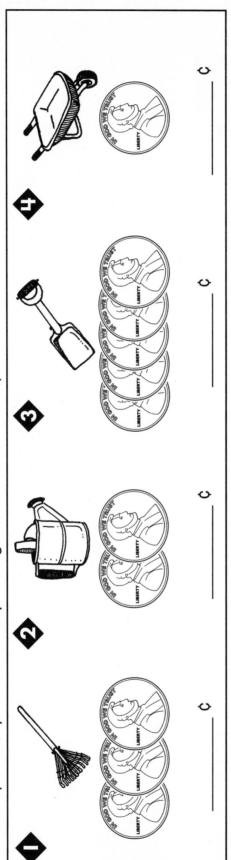

Each child has some pennies to spend at the garden shop. Read the sentences below.
Then write and solve the math problems.

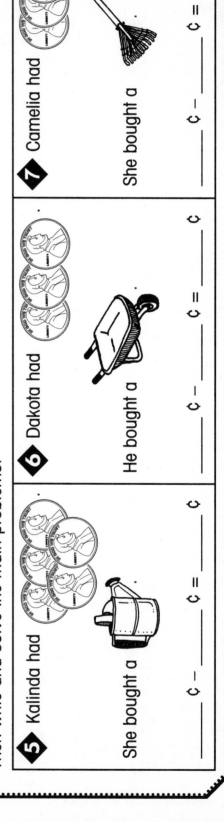

Month-by-Month Math Practice Pages Scholastic Teaching Resources

Name _____

Count the Crop!

Use the chart to answer the questions.

1 How many are in the circle? _____

2 How many  are in the square? _____

3 How many  are in the circle but not in the square? _____

4 How many 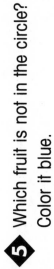 are in the square? _____

5 Which fruit is not in the circle? Color it blue.

Name _____

Apple Snacks

Write the numbers 1, 2, and 3 to put the pictures in order.

1  _____    _____   _____

2 _____   _____   _____

3  _____   _____   _____

4 Circle the tree that has more apples.

5 Circle the picture that does not belong.

Month-by-Month Math Practice Pages   Scholastic Teaching Resources

Name _____

A Day With Apples

On the lines below each clock, write the hour shown on each clock.

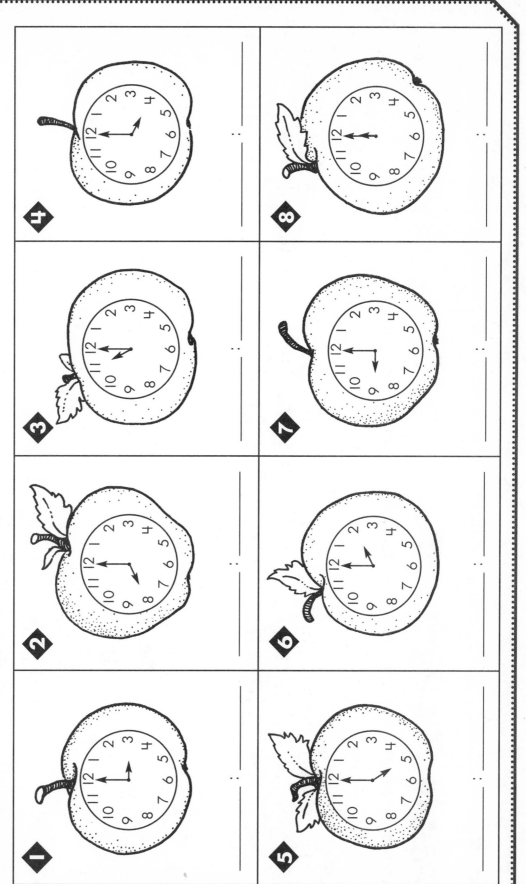

Name _____

Apple Pie Pictures

Look at the pictures. Then write the letter of the picture that matches each sentence.

A.

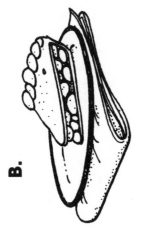

B.

C.

◆ **1** The plate is in front of the cup. ___

◆ **2** The napkin is under the plate. ___

◆ **3** The plate is in between the pie and the napkin. ___

◆ **4** The cup is behind the plate. ___

◆ **5** The plate is on top of the napkin. ___

◆ **6** The apple is beside the pie. ___

◆ **7** The cup is in front of the plate. ___

Month-by-Month Math Practice Pages Scholastic Teaching Resources

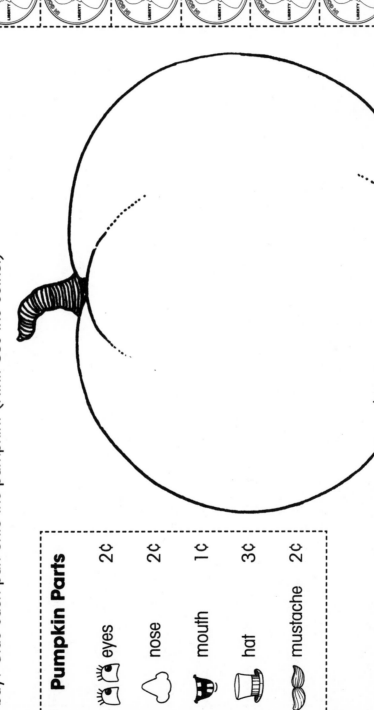

Create a Jack-o'-Lantern!

You have 9¢ to spend on turning this pumpkin into a jack-o'-lantern. Cut out the coins and the jack-o'-lantern parts. What parts can you buy? Glue each part onto the pumpkin. (Hint: Use the coins!)

Pumpkin Parts

eyes		2¢
nose		2¢
mouth		1¢
hat		3¢
mustache		2¢

Name _____

How much money do you have left? I have _____ ¢.

Name _____

On Halloween Night

Draw the hands on the clock to show the time.

1 Devin spent 30 minutes putting on his costume. He started at 6:00. What time did he finish?

2 Tanisha spent 30 minutes bobbing for apples. She finished at 7:00. What time did she start?

3 Lisa went trick-or-treating at 5:00. She returned home half an hour later. What time did she return home?

4 It took Maria half an hour to put on her clown make-up. She finished at 8:30. What time did she start?

5 A trick-or-treater rings the doorbell every half hour. One came at 4:30. When will the next trick-or-treater ring the doorbell?

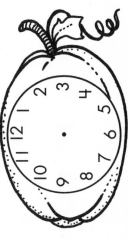

6 Luke spent 30 minutes sorting his candy. He finished at 8:00. What time did he start?

Month-by-Month Math Practice Pages Scholastic Teaching Resources

Scarecrow Numbers

Read each number word. Draw a line from each word to its numeral.

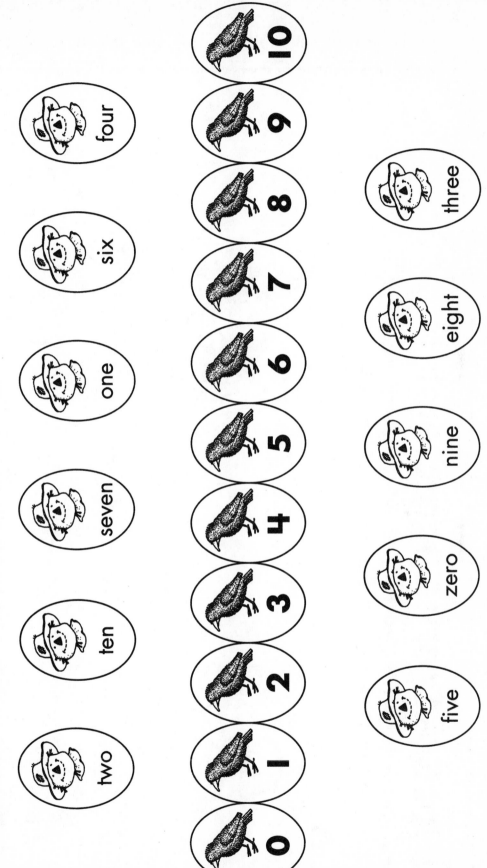

1 2 3 4 5 6 7 8 9 10 11 12 13 14 15 16 17

This is a centimeter ruler. A short way to write **centimeters** is **cm**.

Name _____

(Not So) Scary Characters!

How tall are these trick-or-treaters? Cut out the centimeter ruler and measure the height of both children and the dog. Write each answer on the line.

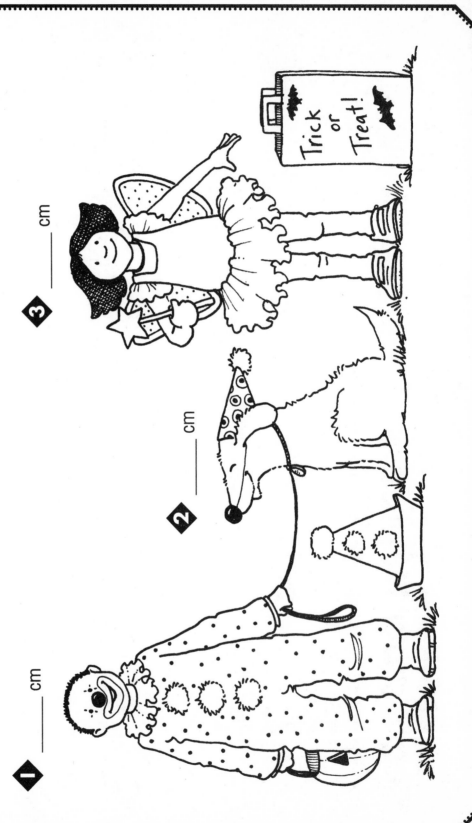

Name _____

Spooky Symmetry

Symmetry is when two halves of an object are the same size and the same shape.
Look at each item and decide if it is symmetrical. Circle **yes** or **no**.

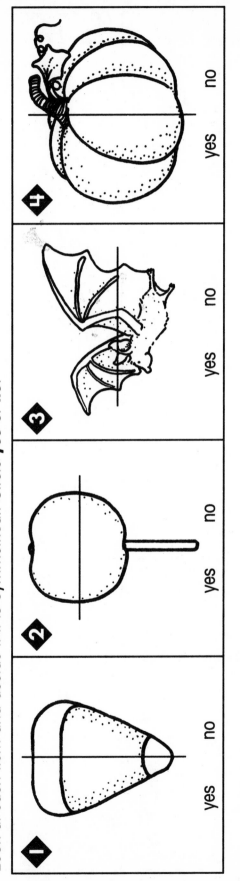

1 yes no

2 yes no

3 yes no

4 yes no

Draw a line to divide each shape into two symmetrical parts.

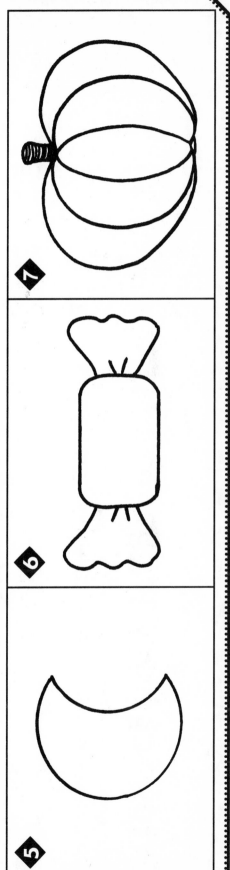

5

6

7

Name _____

What's in the Tree?

Count how many creatures are in each group. Record each number on the graph by coloring in one square for each creature.

1. How many of each creature are there?

2. Are there more  or  ?

3. How many creatures are there in all? _____

Month-by-Month Math Practice Pages Scholastic Teaching Resources

All in a Row

Use ordinal numbers to finish numbering the animals.

1st _____ 2nd _____ _____ 4th _____

1 What animal is 3rd?

2 What animal is after the ?

3 What animal is before the ?

4 What animal is in between the and the ?

5 What animal is 7th?

Tasty Treats

Count how many treats are in each group and write the number.
Which group has more? Circle the number.

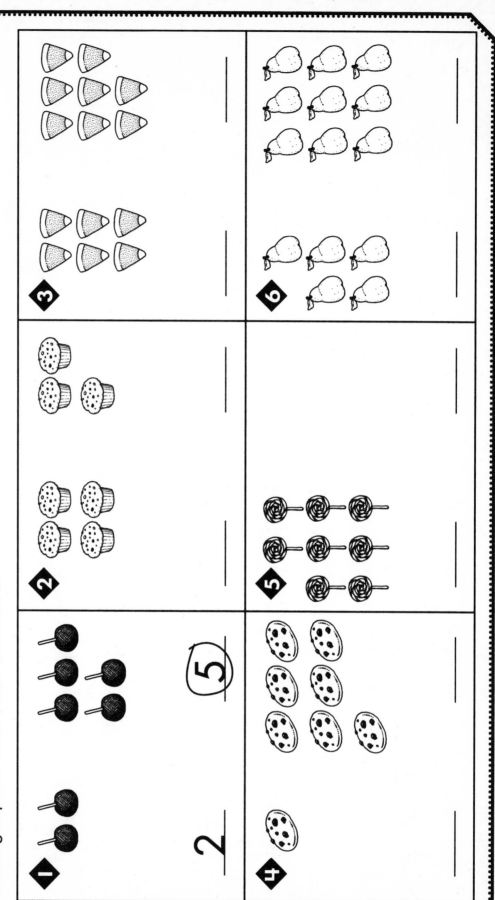

1 — 2

2 — ⑤

3 — ___

4 — ___

5 — ___

6 — ___

Month-by-Month Math Practice Pages Scholastic Teaching Resources

Name _____

Find the Snack!

Find the coordinates of each snack on the graph. Then write the coordinates for each snack on the chart.

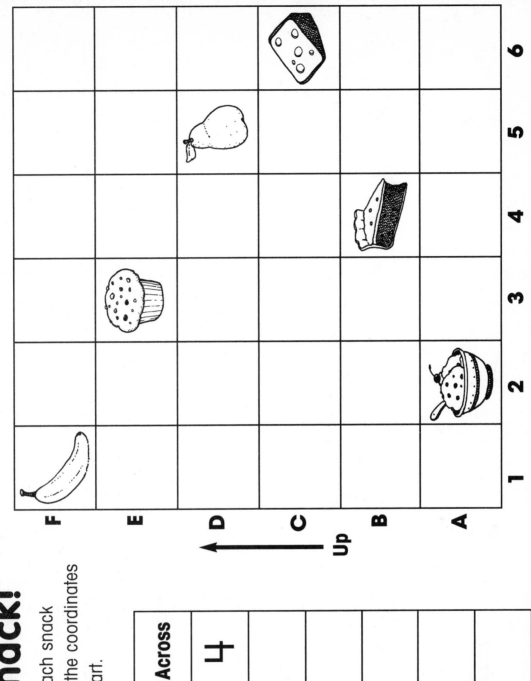

	Up	Across
1.	B	4
2.		
3.		
4.		
5.		
6.		

Name _____

Farm Clues

Follow the directions.

1. Circle the third turkey.

2. Draw a triangle above the first lamb.

3. Draw a line under the first turkey.

4. Draw a square around the first scarecrow.

5. Write a direction to fit one of the remaining pictures.

_____

_____

_____

| 0 | 🦃 | 🦃🦃 | 🦃🦃🦃 | 🦃🦃🦃🦃 | 🦃🦃🦃🦃🦃 |
| 🦃🦃🦃🦃🦃🦃 | 🦃🦃🦃🦃🦃🦃🦃 | 🦃🦃🦃🦃🦃🦃🦃🦃 | 🦃🦃🦃🦃🦃🦃🦃🦃🦃 | 🦃🦃🦃🦃🦃🦃🦃🦃🦃🦃 | 🦃🦃🦃🦃🦃🦃🦃🦃🦃🦃🦃 |

Name _____

Turkey Tally

Cut out the pictures and arrange them to show different ways of making 11.
Glue the pictures in the boxes to make addition sentences.

1 ☐ + ☐ = 11

2 ☐ + ☐ = 11

3 ☐ + ☐ = 11

4 ☐ + ☐ = 11

29

November Numbers

To decode the secret message, write the letter
that goes with each number on the lines.

fourteen	thirteen	twelve	nine	nineteen	fifteen
T	E	I	O	U	R
eighteen	seventeen	twenty	eleven	ten	sixteen
K	D	Y	N	S	L

___ ___ ___ ___ ___ ___
14 19 15 18 13 20

___ ___ ___ ___
10 12 10 15

___ ___ ___
15 19 11

___ ___ ___
19 11 14

___ ___
12 16

___ ___ ___ ___ ___ ___ ___
17 12 11 11 13 13 13

___ ___ ___
17 9 11

___
13 !

Month-by-Month Math Practice Pages Scholastic Teaching Resources

Month-by-Month Math Practice Pages Scholastic Teaching Resources

Name _____

It Happens in November

Use the calendar to follow
the directions below.

Sunday	Monday	Tuesday	Wednesday	Thursday	Friday	Saturday
	1	2	3	4	5	6
7	8	9	10	11	12	13
14	15	16	17	18	19	20
21	22	23	24	25	26	27
28	29	30				

◆1 Thanksgiving is on the fourth
Thursday of the month. Draw a
turkey on that day.

◆2 Election Day is on the first Tuesday
of the month. Draw a red check
mark that day.

◆3 Veterans Day is on November 11th.
Draw a flag on that day.

◆4 Color the Saturdays and Sundays
green.

◆5 When is Thanksgiving Day on this
calendar? Write the date.

_____

Name _____

Color the Cornucopia!

Color the shapes to match the chart. Then answer the questions.

□ = red	
○ = orange	
△ = yellow	
▭ = green	
◇ = blue	
⬠ = purple	

Circle the shape.

1 What shape has three sides? ○ △ □

2 What shape has five sides? ⬠ ○ ◇

Month-by-Month Math Practice Pages Scholastic Teaching Resources

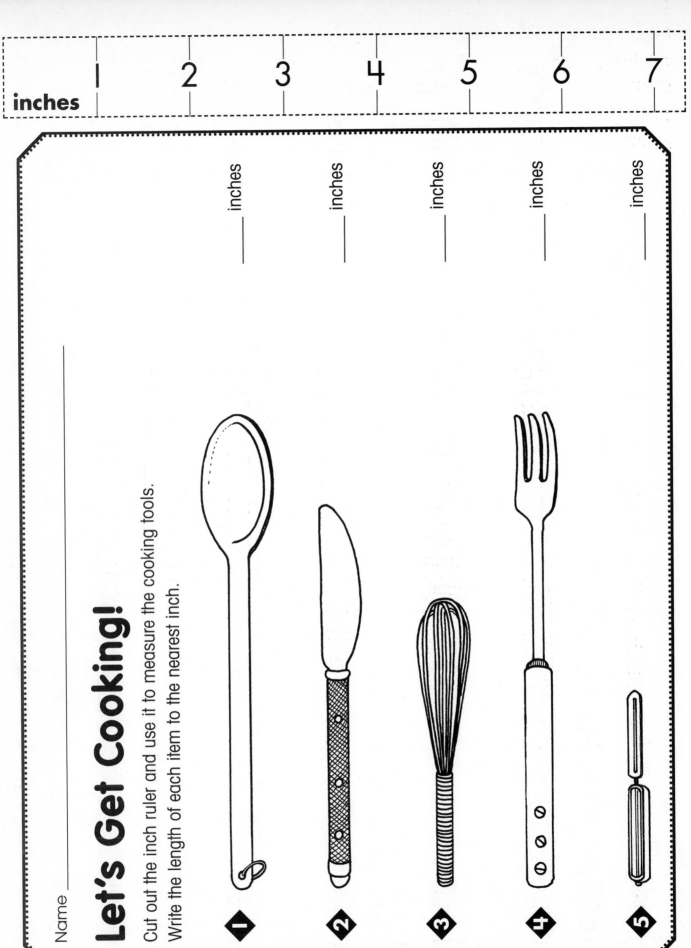

Name _____

Let's Get Cooking!

Cut out the inch ruler and use it to measure the cooking tools.
Write the length of each item to the nearest inch.

1. _____ inches

2. _____ inches

3. _____ inches

4. _____ inches

5. _____ inches

Name _____

After the Harvest

◆ Cut out and arrange the numbers to complete the pattern up to 30. Glue the numbers in place.

5					

Write a sentence describing the pattern.

_____

_____

Write the missing numbers.

2. 20, _____, 30, _____, 40, _____, 50, _____

3. _____, _____, 25, _____, _____, 40, 45, _____

Month-by-Month Math Practice Pages Scholastic Teaching Resources

Candles and Coins

Find the total value of the candles. (Hint: Use the key!)

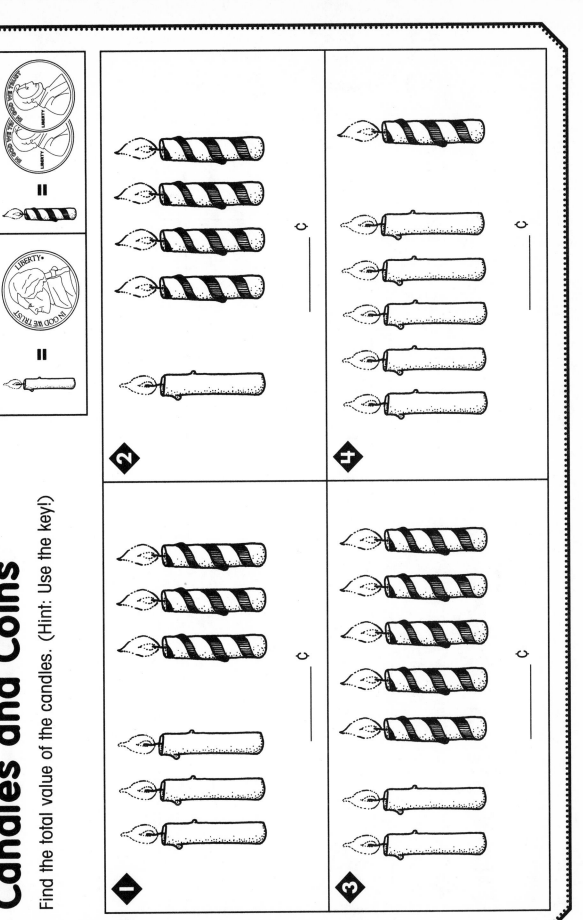

Key

The Colors of Kwanzaa

Name _____

What are the colors of Kwanzaa? To find out, solve each problem, then decode the message.

9 −4	1 +1	3 +6	10 −7	10 −4	5 −4	7 +1	5 −1	6 +1	7 −7
A	D	E	G	L	N	K	R	C	B

To decode the message, write the letter that goes with each number on the line.

___ ___ ___ ' ___ ___ ___ ___ ___
4   9   2   3   4   9   9   1

___ ___ ___ ' ___ ___ ___ ___ ___
5   1   2   0   6   5   7   8

Month-by-Month Math Practice Pages Scholastic Teaching Resources

Month-by-Month Math Practice Pages Scholastic Teaching Resources

Name _____

Decorations Everywhere!

Answer the questions about the graph.

snowflakes	❄	❄	❄	❄	❄	❄	❄		
candy canes	🍬	🍬	🍬	🍬					
stars	☆	☆	☆	☆	☆	☆	☆	☆	☆

1 Are there more snowflakes or more candy canes? _____

2 Are there more stars or snowflakes? _____

3 How many items are there all together? _____

37

Help the Reindeer!

Help this reindeer find his corn! Count by 5s to 100 to color a path for the reindeer to follow.

11	20	25	30	35	90	81	32	17	78
9	15	33	47	40	62	5	23	99	17
5	10	51	41	45	35	82	36	53	93
10	54	87	55	50	52	26	46	17	27
18	63	66	60	31	98	85	90	95	100
7	10	22	77	65	70	75	80	36	
12	15								

Month-by-Month Math Practice Pages Scholastic Teaching Resources

Name _____

Festive Patterns

Color each set of items to make a pattern. Finish labeling each pattern with letters.

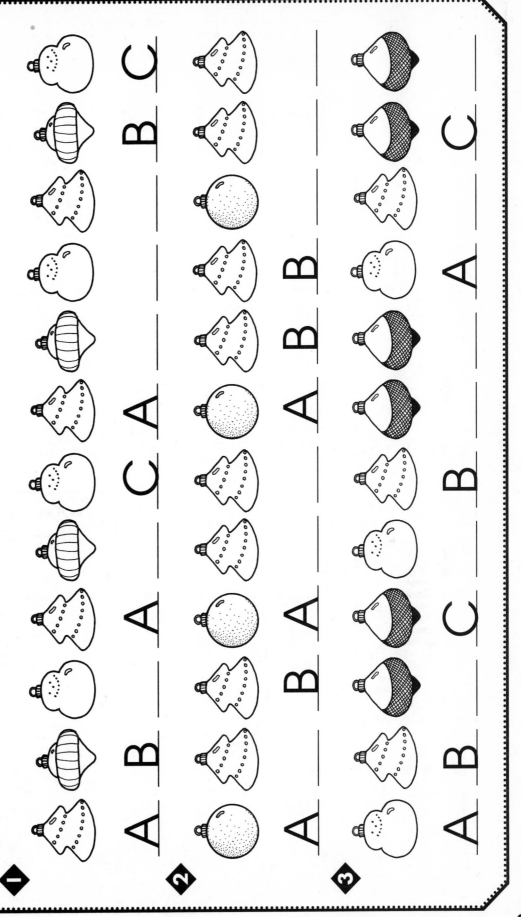

1) A B A B C A B C A B C

2) A B A B A B B A B B

3) A B C A B A B A C

Name _____

Holiday Fractions

Color the shape to show the fraction.

1 $\dfrac{1}{5}$

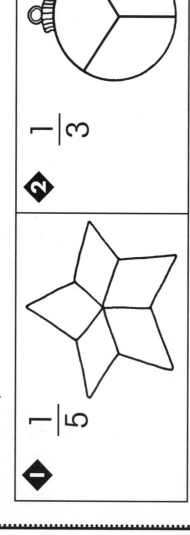

2 $\dfrac{1}{3}$

3 $\dfrac{1}{4}$

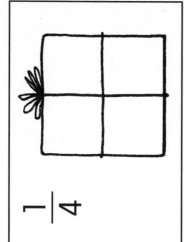

Write the fraction shaded for each shape.

4

5

6

Month-by-Month Math Practice Pages Scholastic Teaching Resources

Gift Boxes

Count the number of square centimeters in each shape.

A

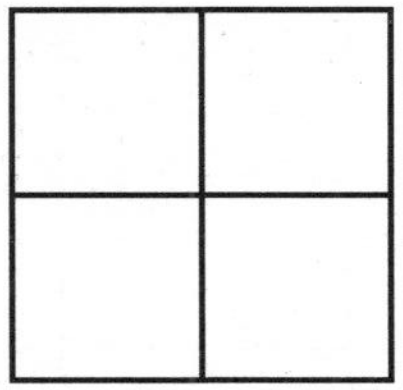

_____ square centimeters

B

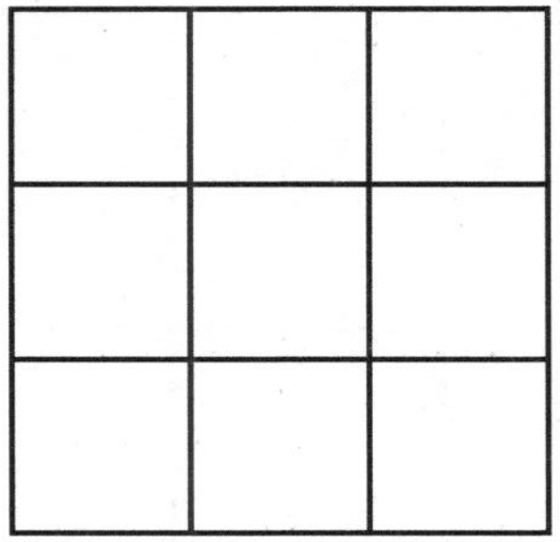

_____ square centimeters

C

_____ square centimeters

D

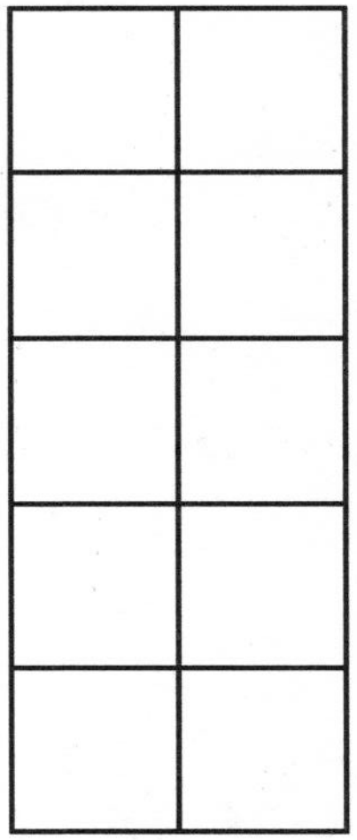

_____ square centimeters

Which gifts fit in which boxes?
Write the letter of the box that fits each gift.

1

Box _____

2

Box _____

3

Box _____

4

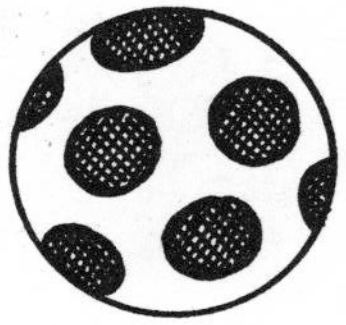

_____ square centimeters

Box _____

Name _____

Gingerbread People

Count the gingerbread people and fill in the graph.

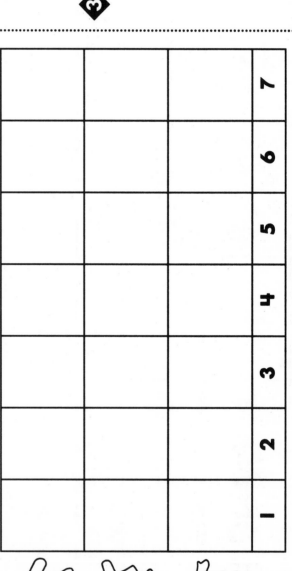

number of gingerbread people

type of gingerbread people

Answer the questions.
Circle the correct answer.

1 Are there more

or ?

2 Are there more

or ?

3 How many gingerbread
people are there
all together?

_____

Month-by-Month Math Practice Pages   Scholastic Teaching Resources

Name _____

Winter Wear

Color the clothes in the key below.
Then use the colors in the key to make
as many different outfits as you can.

How many different outfits can
Wesley make?

Key

red	orange	yellow
green	blue	purple

Wesley can make _____
different outfits.

Color Wesley's
clothes to match
your favorite outfit.

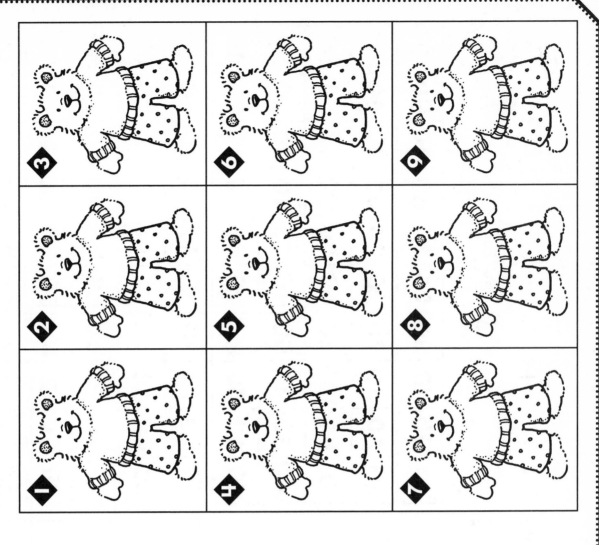

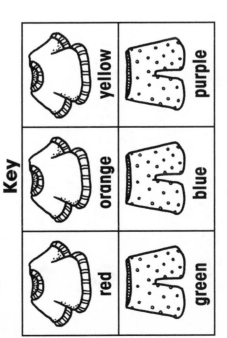

Name _____

Making Hundreds

Solve the math problems below.
Then color pairs of numbers in the grid
that equal 100. Use a different color
crayon for each pair.

10	90	10	30	20	30	60	40	40	0
20	50	50	70	20	80	30	40	50	100
0	40	100	50	60	60	90	10	70	30
100	30	0	50	40	70	70	80	20	50
40	60	30	100	20	30	40	60	80	20
10	20	70	10	0	10	80	30	60	10
60	40	30	90	0	100	90	70	70	90
0	10	10	60	100	40	60	80	80	60
30	90	0	100	50	90	100	0	20	90
70	10	100	10	50	20	80	80	80	10

1 ◆ 0 + _____ = 100

2 ◆ _____ + 90 = 100

3 ◆ 20 + _____ = 100

4 ◆ _____ + 70 = 100

5 ◆ 40 + _____ = 100

6 ◆ _____ + 50 = 100

7 ◆ 60 + _____ = 100

Month-by-Month Math Practice Pages Scholastic Teaching Resources

Name _____

Cold Weather Animals

Use the graph to answer the questions.

◆ **1** Which animal is the longest?

_____

◆ **2** Which two animals are about the same size?

_____

◆ **3** About how long is the fox?

_____

◆ **4** Which animal is shorter than the fox?

_____

◆ **5** Which animals are more than 5 feet long?

_____

length in feet

| | Whale | Fox | Polar Bear | Penguin | Walrus |

type of animal

Martin Luther King, Jr.

1929 Born in Atlanta, Georgia	**1948** Graduated from Morehouse College	**1964** Civil Rights Act signed	**1965** Voting Rights Act signed

1944 Started college

1963 Gave the I Have a Dream speech

1964 Awarded the Nobel Peace Prize

Use the time line to answer the questions.

◆ 1 How old was Martin Luther King, Jr. when he started college? _____

◆ 2 What two events happened in 1964? _____

and _____

◆ 3 What year did Martin Luther King, Jr. give the I Have a Dream speech? _____

Name Patterns

Read and follow the clues to discover a secret pattern.

Clues

- Write your first name in the boxes, one letter per box.

- Continue writing your first name in the boxes until the grid is complete. Do not skip any boxes.

- Color each letter of your name a different color. (For example, you might make all the **A**s red and all the **B**s blue.)

Describe the color pattern. _____

Counting by 10s

Find and color each word in the word search.

o	n	e	h	u	n	d	r	e	d
v	l	t	u	f	e	g	f	i	c
k	e	s	d	m	e	h	i	n	f
t	w	e	n	t	y	z	f	i	t
m	s	v	c	y	d	f	t	n	h
j	a	e	i	g	h	t	y	e	i
d	x	n	b	z	n	r	m	t	r
w	i	t	s	i	x	t	y	y	t
a	k	y	o	c	h	e	j	a	y
f	o	r	t	y	p	n	b	q	g

◆1 ten

◆2 twenty

◆3 thirty

◆4 forty

◆5 fifty

◆6 sixty

◆7 seventy

◆8 eighty

◆9 ninety

◆10 one hundred

Name _____

Snowman Math

Spin the spinner.
Write a + or − sign in the box
beside each snowman.
Then solve the problem.

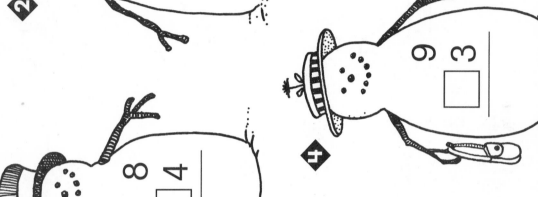

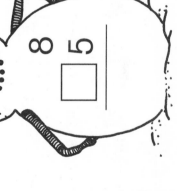

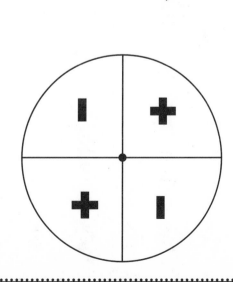

1
8
□ 4
___

2
1
□ 1
___

3
8
□ 5
___

4
9
□ 3
___

5
4
□ 1
___

Make a spinner
using a paper clip
and a pencil.

Name _____

Mittens on the Clothesline

Write each set of numbers in the correct order from smallest to largest.

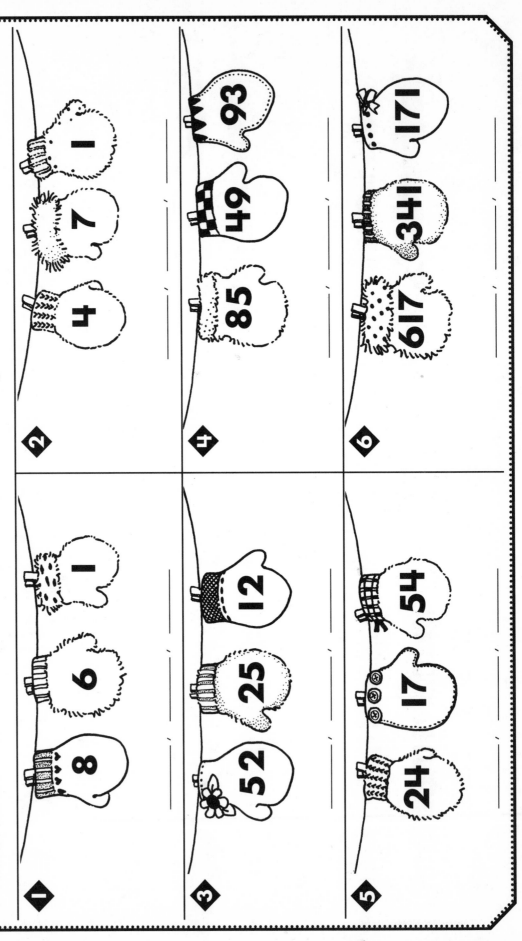

◆ 1

8   6   1

◆ 2

4   7   1

◆ 3

52   25   12

◆ 4

85   49   93

◆ 5

24   17   54

◆ 6

617   341   171

Name _____

Valentine Cards

Read the clues to find each child's card.
If a card does not fit the clue, make an **X** on that card.

Clues

1. Mike draws happy
faces on his cards.

2. Rita makes cards that
look like puzzles.

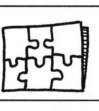

3. Maria draws hearts
on her cards.

Draw lines matching each person
to his or her card.

Rita

Mike

Maria

Name _____

Sweethearts

Using the key, count the number of tens and ones.
Write how many there are on the lines.

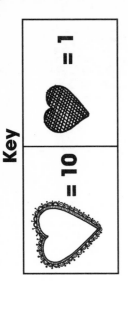

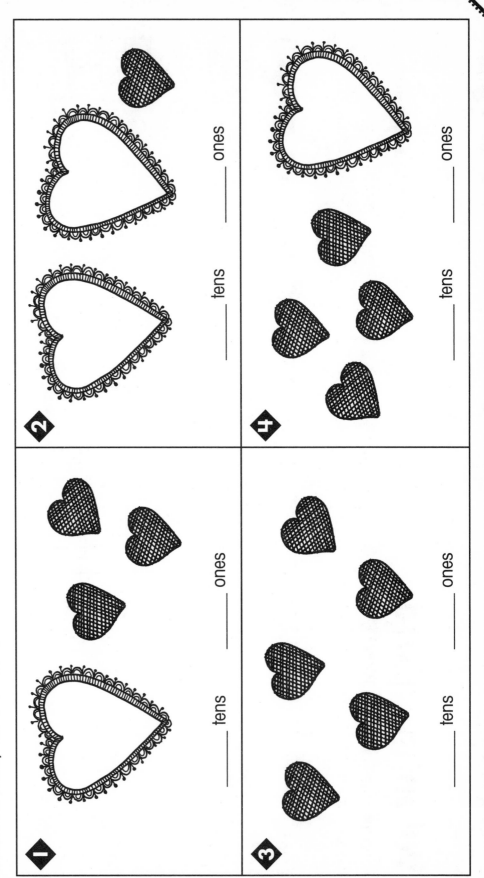

1

_____ tens

_____ ones

2

_____ tens

_____ ones

3

_____ tens

_____ ones

4

_____ tens

_____ ones

Name _____

Three in a Line

Follow the directions to color three hearts in a straight line. Roll two dice. Add or subtract the numbers that appear on top of each die. Write the problem, **+** or **–**, and answer on the lines. Color any heart on the board that matches your answer. Color three hearts in a line. (Hint: The line can be horizontal, vertical, or diagonal!)

0	9	6	7	1
12	5	6	12	6
7	2	4	5	8
8	3	2	7	0
1	11	4	9	8
5	2	9	10	4

___ ___ = ___

___ ___ = ___

___ ___ = ___

___ ___ = ___

___ ___ = ___

___ ___ = ___

___ ___ = ___

Name _____

Fact Families

Use the numbers on each valentine to make two addition problems and two subtraction problems.

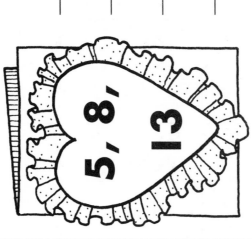

3, 4, 7

____ + ____ = ____

____ + ____ = ____

____ - ____ = ____

____ - ____ = ____

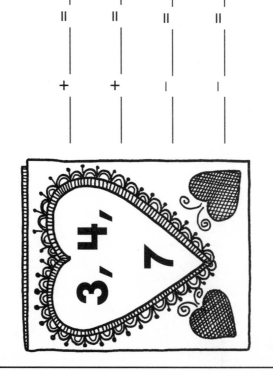

5, 8, 13

____ + ____ = ____

____ + ____ = ____

____ - ____ = ____

____ - ____ = ____

Count by 2s. Write the missing numbers in each row.

2	4	____	____	10	____	____	____	____	____
____	____	____	____	____	20	____	____	____	48
26	____	____	____	____	____	38	____	____	____

Name _____

With Minutes to Go!

Circle the minutes shown on each clock.

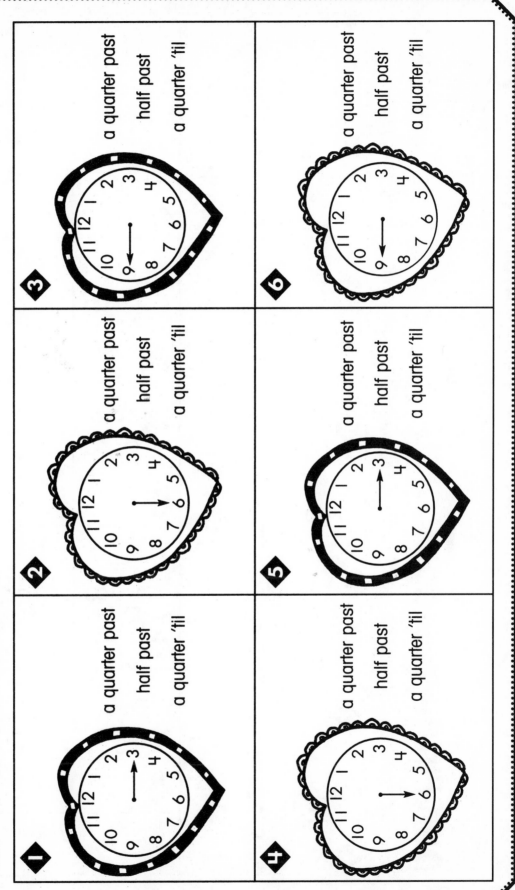

1
a quarter past
half past
a quarter 'til

2
a quarter past
half past
a quarter 'til

3
a quarter past
half past
a quarter 'til

4
a quarter past
half past
a quarter 'til

5
a quarter past
half past
a quarter 'til

6
a quarter past
half past
a quarter 'til

Our First President

Solve each problem. To decode the secret message, write the letter that goes with each number on the line.

1.
$$10 + 3$$
A

2.
$$12 - 7$$
E

3.
$$8 + 4$$
G

4.
$$14 - 3$$
H

5.
$$7 - 3$$
I

6.
$$14 - 4$$
N

7.
$$12 + 2$$
O

8.
$$17 - 8$$
R

9.
$$12 - 6$$
S

10.
$$17 - 9$$
T

11.
$$15 - 8$$
W

___ ___ ___ ___ ___ ___ ___ ___ ___ ___ ___ ___ ___ ___ ___
12 5 14 9 12 5   7 13 6 11 4 10 12 8 14 10

Month-by-Month Math Practice Pages Scholastic Teaching Resources

Name _____

Our 16th President

Help Abraham Lincoln find his hat. Color only the spaces that have 16 as the answer.

9 + 7	7 + 7	2 + 7	16 − 4	10 + 2
15 + 1	5 + 11	17 − 1	2 + 14	16 − 6
12 − 5	15 − 8	12 + 0	13 + 3	3 + 8
10 + 5	13 + 3	4 + 12	20 − 4	13 − 3
10 + 0	17 − 1	17 + 9	11 + 7	10 − 1
13 − 1	16 + 0	19 − 3	8 + 8	11 + 5

Dental Health Supplies

You have 90¢ to spend at the pharmacy.

Make a list of what you will buy and how much money you will have left. (Hint: Cut out and use the coins!)

Name _____

toothbrush 20¢

toothpaste 40¢

mirror 30¢   mouthwash 50¢

dental floss 10¢

I will buy: It costs:

_____   _____ ¢

_____   _____ ¢

_____   _____ ¢

_____   _____ ¢

Total amount spent:

I will have _____ ¢ left.

Month-by-Month Math Practice Pages Scholastic Teaching Resources

Name _____

Lively Leprechauns

Which leprechaun is which? Look at the pictures. Write the letter of the picture that matches each sentence.

A.

B.

C.

◆1 I am wearing a hat. I am holding a three-leaf clover. Which leprechaun am I? _____

◆2 I have a clover on my hat. I am wearing a bow tie. Which leprechaun am I? _____

◆3 I am dancing a jig. I am wearing boots. Which leprechaun am I? _____

◆4 I am wearing a belt. I have some coins. Which leprechaun am I? _____

◆5 I have a buckle on my hat. I am sitting. Which leprechaun am I? _____

Pots of Gold

Draw a line from each set of bills to its dollar value.

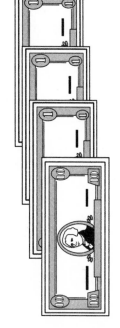

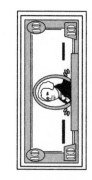

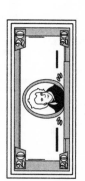

$7

$13

$10

$20

$5

Month-by-Month Math Practice Pages Scholastic Teaching Resources

Name _____

Spot the Pattern!

Circle the mistake in each pattern. Draw the correct picture on the line.

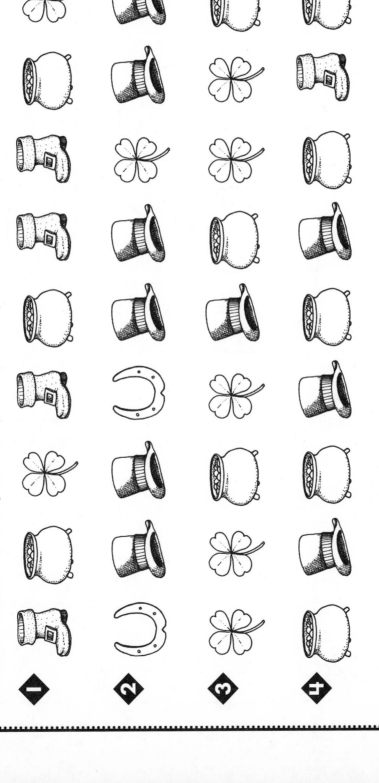

Draw shapes to make your own pattern.

Lucky Fractions

Color the shape to show the fraction.

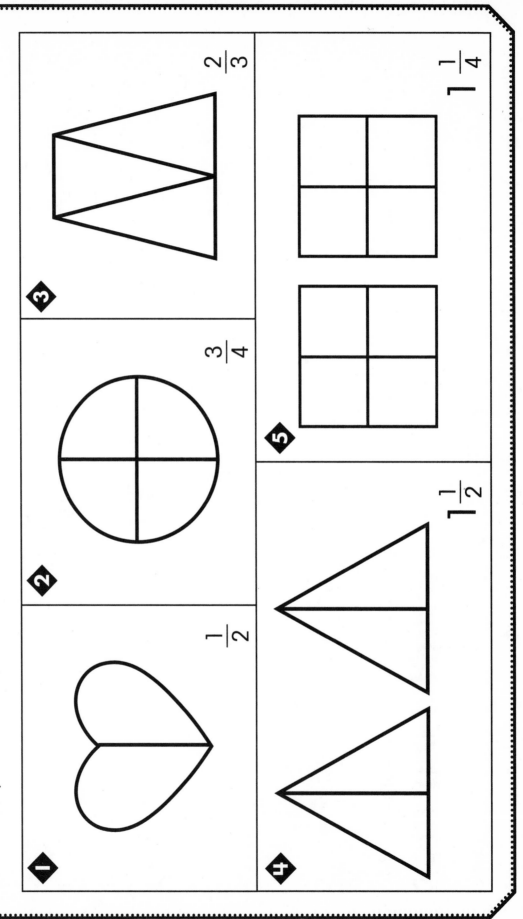

1 $\frac{1}{2}$

2 $\frac{3}{4}$

3 $\frac{2}{3}$

4 $1\frac{1}{2}$

5 $1\frac{1}{4}$

Month-by-Month Math Practice Pages Scholastic Teaching Resources

Name _____

Weather Report

Read the weather reports and record the dates. Then complete the calendar by drawing pictures to show the weather. Use the legend for reference.

Weather Reports

1 It rained on the third Monday. _____

2 It snowed on the last Saturday of the month. _____

3 It was cloudy the entire second week of the month. _____

4 It was sunny on the first day of the month. _____

5 It rained on the last Thursday of the month. _____

Sunday	Monday	Tuesday	Wednesday	Thursday	Friday	Saturday
		1	2	3	4	5
6	7	8	9	10	11	12
13	14	15	16	17	18	19
20	21	22	23	24	25	26
27	28	29	30	31		

Legend

cloudy	snowy	sunny	rainy

Name _____

Colorful Kites

Solve each problem. Use your answers to color the kites. (Hint: Use the key!)

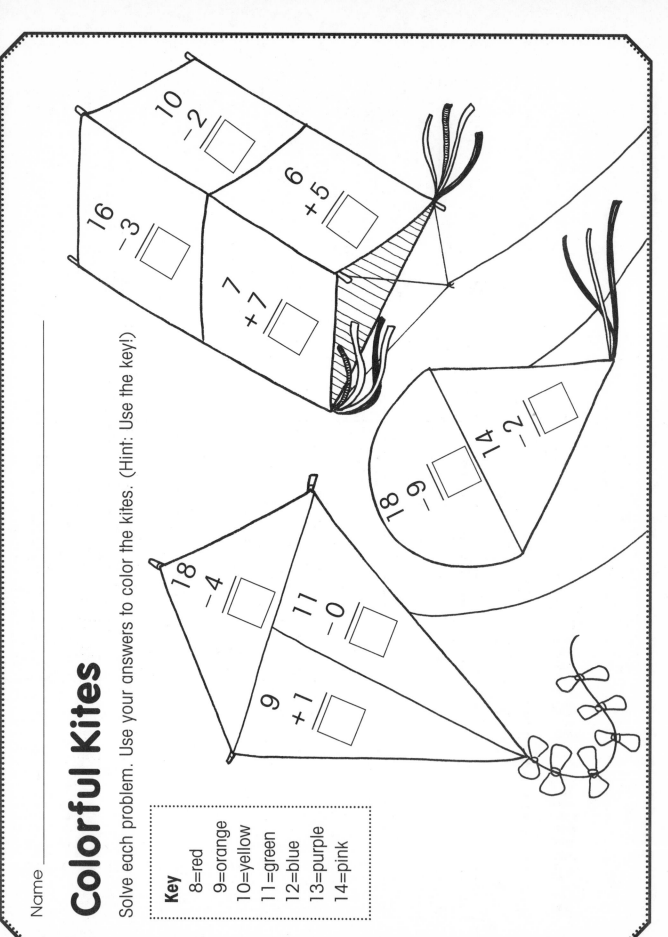

$$10 - 2 = \boxed{}$$

$$16 - 3 = \boxed{}$$

$$6 + 5 = \boxed{}$$

$$7 + 7 = \boxed{}$$

$$18 - 9 = \boxed{}$$

$$14 - 2 = \boxed{}$$

$$18 - 4 = \boxed{}$$

$$11 - 0 = \boxed{}$$

$$9 + 1 = \boxed{}$$

Key
8=red
9=orange
10=yellow
11=green
12=blue
13=purple
14=pink

Month-by-Month Math Practice Pages Scholastic Teaching Resources

Name _____

Flower Petals

Color the flower petals to make a beautiful garden:
Color the petals with even numbers red.
Color the petals with odd numbers yellow.

Name _____

Spring Happenings

Write the numbers 1, 2, and 3 to put the pictures in order.

1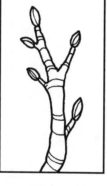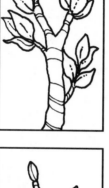

_____ _____ _____

2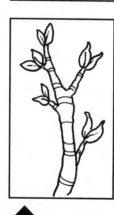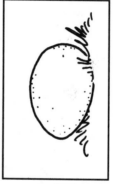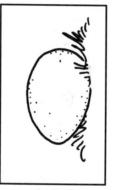

_____ _____ _____

3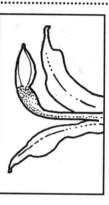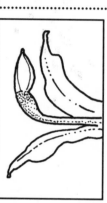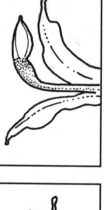

_____ _____ _____

4 Circle the picture that does not belong.

Month-by-Month Math Practice Pages Scholastic Teaching Resources

Name _____

Fishing Season

Look at the number on the fish.
Circle all the problems with answers that match this number.

1 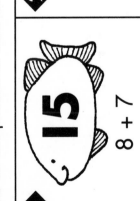 **15** 8 + 7 6 + 9 16 – 1 17 – 0	**2** **18** 18 – 0 9 + 9 5 + 13 10 + 9	**3** **17** 11 + 6 9 + 8 5 + 10 16 – 3	**4** **12** 19 – 7 18 – 7 12 – 6 6 + 6
5 **14** 4 + 11 9 + 4 7 + 7 19 – 5	**6** **16** 8 + 8 18 – 2 3 + 13 19 – 3	**7** **13** 5 + 8 7 + 7 14 – 4 12 + 1	**8** **11** 17 – 6 6 + 6 5 – 5 1 + 1

Bunny Math

Use the number line to solve each problem.

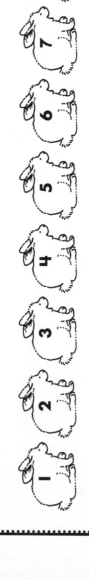

1 4
+6
☐

2 6
+6
☐

3 2
+10
☐

4 7
+4
☐

5 9
+3
☐

6 1
+9
☐

7 5
+7
☐

8 3
+8
☐

9 8
+4
☐

10 2
+9
☐

Month-by-Month Math Practice Pages Scholastic Teaching Resources

Name _____

The Egg Mystery

Look at the eggs and read each clue. Write the letter of the animal that matches each clue.

A

B

C

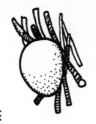

D

1

I am a bird that cannot fly.

I lay the largest egg.

It is 6 inches tall.

Which animal am I? _____

2

I am a bird that can hunt at night.

I sometimes lay my eggs in hollow trees.

Which animal am I? _____

3

I am a reptile with a hard shell on my back.

I lay my eggs near water in mud or sand.

Which animal am I? _____

4

I am a bird you may see on a farm.

I lay my eggs in a hen house.

Which animal am I? _____

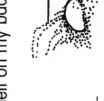

Name ___

Mopsy's Garden

Cut out the pictures and read each clue. Glue the pictures where they belong in Mopsy's garden.

Legend

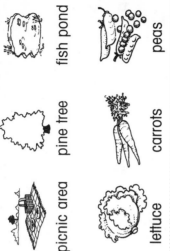

picnic area   pine tree   fish pond   campsite

lettuce   carrots   peas   corn

1. The lettuce is planted west of Mopsy.
2. The carrots are planted east of the picnic area.
3. The corn is planted north of the lettuce.
4. The peas are planted south of the fish pond.

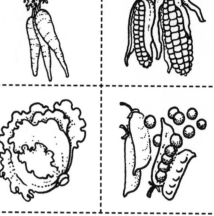

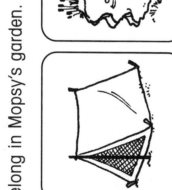

Month-by-Month Math Practice Pages Scholastic Teaching Resources

Name _____

More Than a Dozen

Use the chart to answer the questions.

◆1 How many are in the oval? _____

◆2 How many are in the rectangle? _____

◆3 How many are in both the oval and the rectangle? _____

◆4 How many are in the oval? _____

◆5 Which picture is in the oval, in the rectangle, and in both the oval and the rectangle? Color it orange.

Name _____

Let's Recycle!

Count the recyclable items and color in one square in the graph for each.

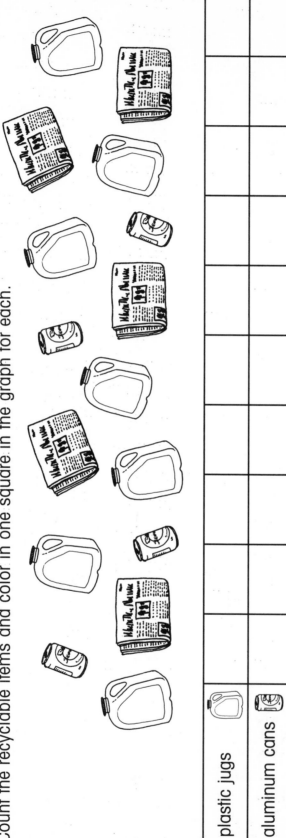

	1	2	3	4	5	6	7	8	9	10
plastic jugs										
aluminum cans										
newspapers										

Write answers to the questions.

◆1 Are there more newspapers or plastic jugs? _____

◆2 Are there more aluminum cans or newspapers? _____

◆3 Which item is there the least of? _____

Month-by-Month Math Practice Pages Scholastic Teaching Resources

Name _____

Will It Happen Today?

Read each set of statements. Which event is more likely to happen today? Circle that statement.

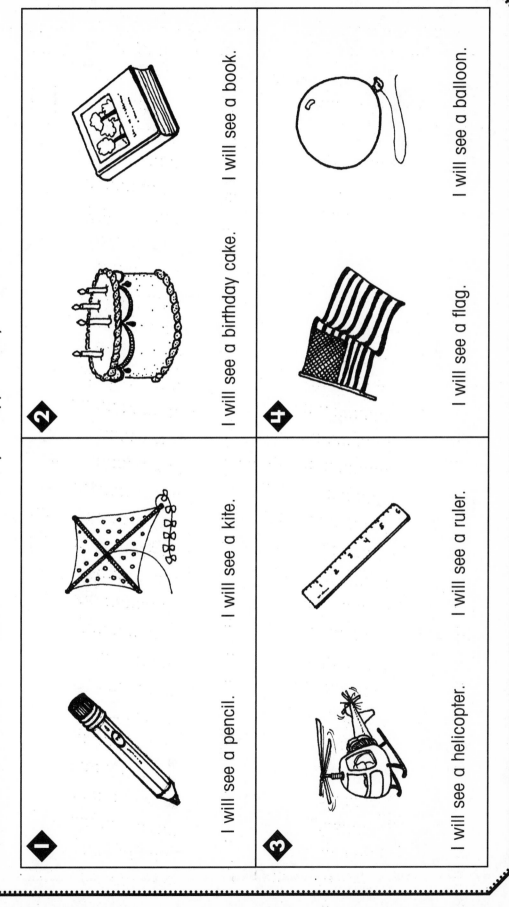

1

I will see a pencil.

I will see a kite.

2

I will see a birthday cake.

I will see a book.

3

I will see a helicopter.

I will see a ruler.

4

I will see a flag.

I will see a balloon.

Name _____

Give Me Five!

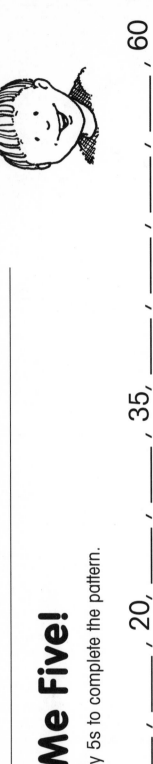

◆1 Count by 5s to complete the pattern.

5, _____, 20, _____, 35, _____, _____, 60

◆2 Count by 5s to find
the number of minutes
in each hour.
Write the correct
number of minutes
in each box.

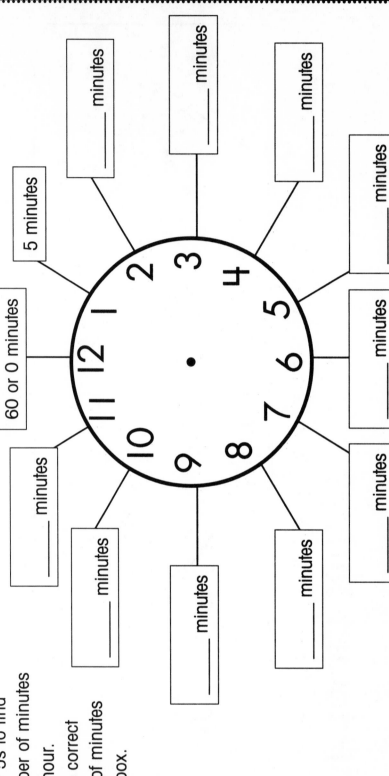

_____ minutes

_____ minutes

_____ minutes

_____ minutes

5 minutes

60 or 0 minutes

_____ minutes

_____ minutes

_____ minutes

_____ minutes

_____ minutes

Month-by-Month Math Practice Pages Scholastic Teaching Resources

Name _____

Making Bouquets

Circle sets of 3.

1 9 ÷ 3 = _____ in each set.

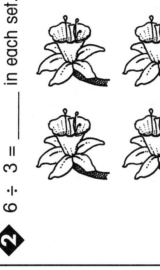

2 6 ÷ 3 = _____ in each set.

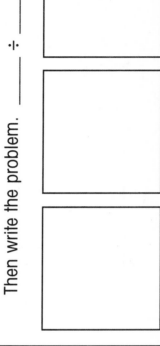

3 15 ÷ 3= _____ in each set.

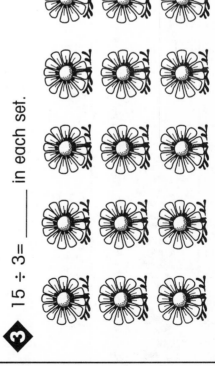

4 Draw 12 triangles in 3 sets.

Then write the problem. _____ ÷ _____ = _____

75

Name _____

It's Spring!

Solve the problems. To decode the secret message, write the letter that goes with each number on the lines.

$5+9$	$10-6$	$6+3$	$11-4$	$18+2$	$13-7$	$3+15$	$12-9$
I	Y	A	W	O	H	E	B
$9+1$	$15-2$	$9+8$	$20-9$	$4+12$	$15-7$	$12+3$	$8+4$
N	G	P	F	M	R	L	S

___ ___ ___ ___ ___   ___ ___ ___ ___ ___ ___ ___
9 17 8 14 15   12 6 20 7 18 8 12

___ ___ ___ ___ ___   ___ ___ ___   ___ ___ ___ ___ ___ ___ ___
3 8 14 10 13   16 9 4   11 15 20 7 18 8 12

Month-by-Month Math Practice Pages   Scholastic Teaching Resources

Name _____

Green Thumbs

Cut out the pictures and glue them in order on the time line.

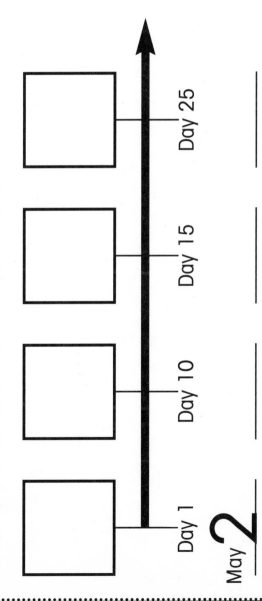

Day 1   Day 10   Day 15   Day 25

May

Sunday	Monday	Tuesday	Wednesday	Thursday	Friday	Saturday
	1	2	3	4	5	6
7	8	9	10	11	12	13
14	15	16	17	18	19	20
21	22	23	24	25	26	27
28	29	30	31			

The seed was
planted on May 2.

Use the calendar to
write the dates for
the other events
on the lines above.

May 2

1 What day of the week was
the seed planted?

_____

2 What day of the week did
the leaves appear?

_____

3 What day of the week did
the flower bloom?

_____

77

Name _____

Sport Shop

How much money does each item cost? Write the value of the coins under each picture.

_____   _____   _____   _____   _____

Answer each question.

1 Zachary has 75¢. He buys a basketball. How much money does he have left? _____ ¢

2 Sarah has $1.25. She buys a bike helmet. How much money does she have left? _____ ¢

3 Brian has 25¢. What can he buy? _____

4 Jill has 50¢. Does she have enough money to buy a fishing pole?

   Circle the answer.   Yes   No

Month-by-Month Math Practice Pages Scholastic Teaching Resources

Name _____

Memorial Day Parade

Read the clues to find out who carried what item in the parade.

If an item does not fit the clue, make an **X** on that item.

Clues

1. Lisa enjoys playing
with balloons.

2. Alex enjoys waving flags.

3. Paula enjoys playing
musical instruments.

Draw lines matching each person
to the item he or she carried.

Paula

Alex

Lisa

In the Neighborhood

Use the map to answer the questions. Circle the answer.
(Hint: Use the compass rose to find north, south, east and west.)

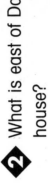

N E S W compass rose

Cara's house	PETS pet shop	Latoya's house
ice rink	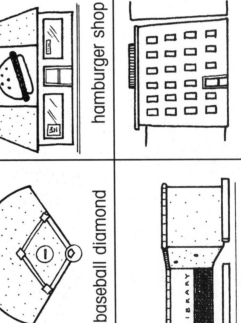 baseball diamond	hamburger shop
Damon's house	 library	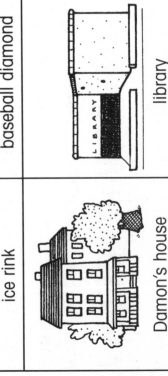 Omar's house

1 What is north of the baseball diamond?

   pet shop   ice rink

2 What is east of Damon's house?

   library   Cara's house

3 What is south of the hamburger shop?

   Omar's house
   Latoya's house

4 What is north of the library?

   baseball diamond

   ice rink

Month-by-Month Math Practice Pages Scholastic Teaching Resources

Name _____

Flower Care

Read the statements and answer the questions by drawing the hour and minute hands to show the time.

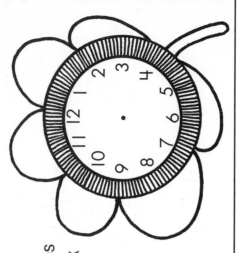

1 Gus started watering the garden at 6:00. It took half an hour.

What time did Gus finish watering the garden?

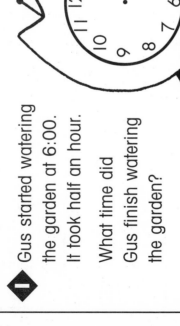

2 Jessica started pruning the roses at 10:15. It took 30 minutes.

What time did Jessica finish pruning the roses?

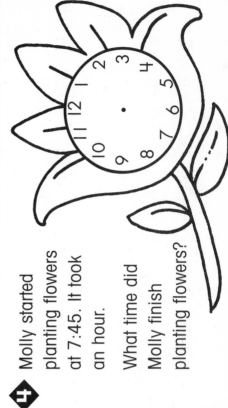

3 Derek started raking leaves at 3:30. It took a quarter of an hour.

What time did Derek finish raking leaves?

4 Molly started planting flowers at 7:45. It took an hour.

What time did Molly finish planting flowers?

Plenty of Plants

Read each word problem and draw the correct number of flowers in each pot.
Write the addition problem and the multiplication problem for each word problem.

1 Nora had 2 pots. She planted 1 sunflower in each pot.

How many sunflowers are there in all?

____ + ____ = ☐ ☐

____ x ____ = ☐ ☐

2 Colby had 3 pots. He planted 2 carnations in each pot.

How many carnations are there in all?

____ + ____ + ____ = ☐

____ x ____ = ☐

3 Maya had 2 pots. She planted 3 violets in each pot.

How many violets are there in all?

____ + ____ = ☐ ☐

____ x ____ = ☐ ☐

Name _____

Tie Patterns

Use letters to finish labeling each pattern.

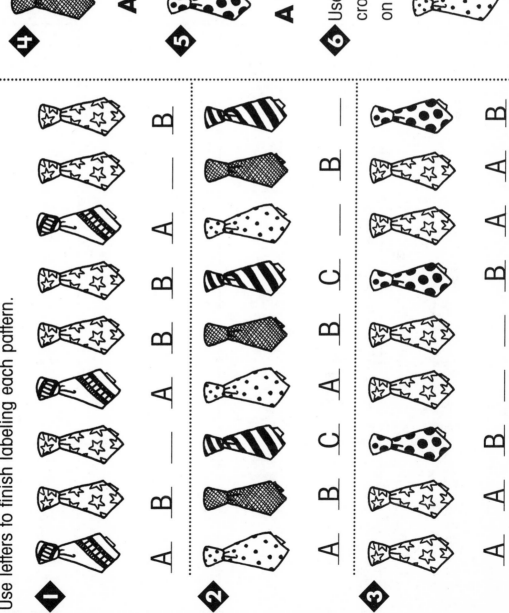

1 A B __ A __ B B A __

2 A B C A B C __ __ B

3 A A B __ __ B A A B

Look at each pattern. What kind of pattern is it? Circle the answer.

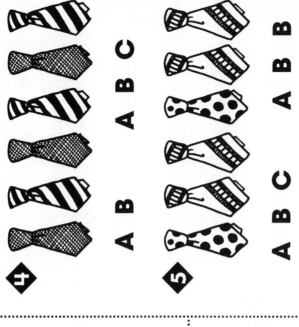

4 A B   A B C

5 A B C   A B B

6 Use red, yellow, and blue crayons to color an ABC pattern on the ties below.

Nick's Busy June

Read the questions and record the dates. (Hint: Use the legend!)

Sunday	Monday	Tuesday	Wednesday	Thursday	Friday	Saturday
1 	2 	3 	4	5	6	7
8 	9 	10 	11 	12	13	14
15	16	17	18	19	20	21
22	23	24	25	26	27	28
29	30					

Legend

birthday	vacation	Flag Day	baseball	library

1 What day of the week will Nick go to the library?

_____

2 What day of the week will Nick play baseball?

_____

3 When is Flag Day? Write the date.

_____

4 How many days will Nick be on vacation?

_____

5 What day is Nick's birthday?

_____

Month-by-Month Math Practice Pages Scholastic Teaching Resources

Name _____

Safe and Sound

Make a graph showing safety equipment. Count the items and color one square in the graph for each.

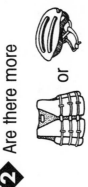

type of safety equipment							
	I	2	3	4	5	6	7

number of items

Circle the answer to each question.

1 Are there more or ?

2 Are there more or 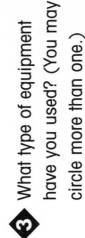 ?

3 What type of equipment have you used? (You may circle more than one.)

Warm-Weather Weights

Circle the object that weighs more.

Use the numbers 1, 2, and 3 to order the objects from lightest to heaviest.

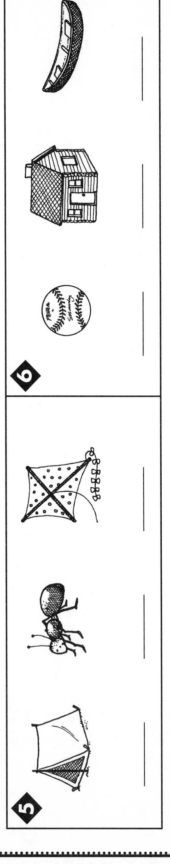

6 Name something that is heavier than you. _____

7 Name something that is lighter than you. _____

Month-by-Month Math Practice Pages Scholastic Teaching Resources

Name _____

How Tall?

Which item is taller in real life? Circle it.

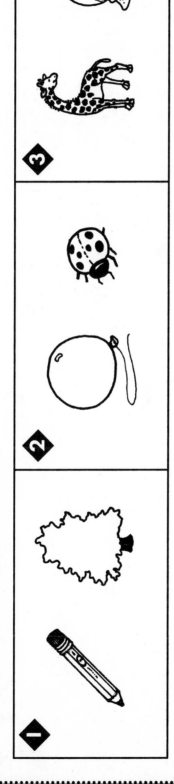

Use the numbers 1, 2, and 3 to order the objects from shortest to tallest.

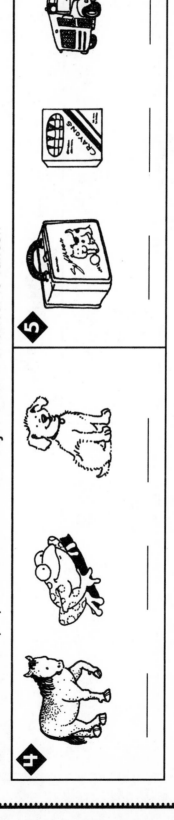

6 Name something that is taller than you. _____

7 Name something that is shorter than you. _____

Name _____

Snack Time

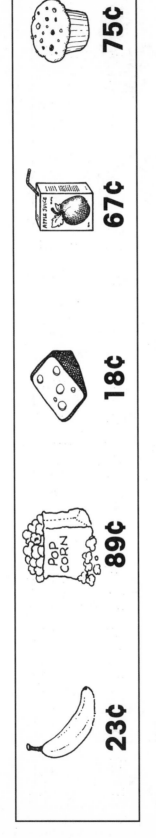

| 23¢ | 89¢ | 18¢ | 67¢ | 75¢ |

Use the numbers 1, 2, and 3 to number the snacks from least expensive to most expensive.

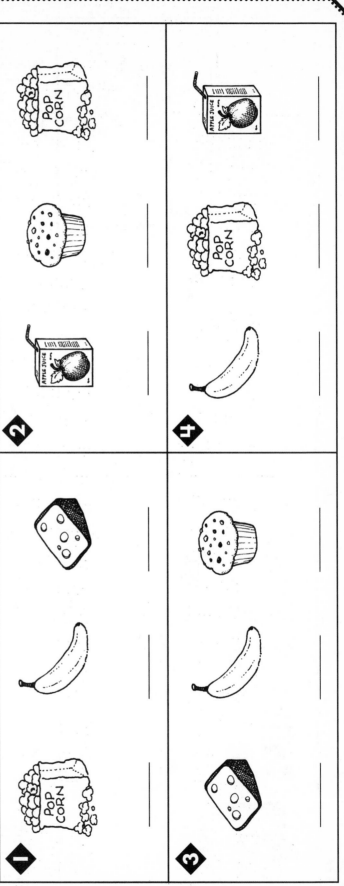

1 (popcorn, banana, cheese)

2 (apple juice, muffin, popcorn)

3 (cheese, banana, muffin)

4 (banana, popcorn, apple juice)

Month-by-Month Math Practice Pages Scholastic Teaching Resources

Month-by-Month Math Practice Pages   Scholastic Teaching Resources

Name _____

Multiplication Riddles

Compete and solve each multiplication problem.

1 Each dog has four legs. How many legs are there on three dogs?

4 x _____ = _____

2 Each spider has eight legs. How many legs are there on two spiders?

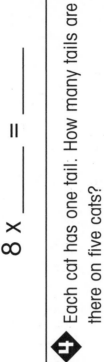

8 x _____ = _____

3 Each bat has two wings. How many wings are there on four bats?

2 x _____ = _____

4 Each cat has one tail. How many tails are there on five cats?

1 x _____ = _____

Name _____

Riverbank Division

Write the division problem for each set of animals. Complete the sentence to check your answer.

1 Eight fish in two groups.

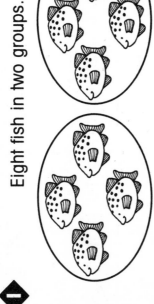

$8 \div 2 =$ _____

There are _____ fish in each group.

2 Three ducks in three groups.

$3 \div 3 =$ _____

There is _____ duck in each group.

3 Ten turtles in two groups.

$10 \div 2 =$ _____

There are _____ turtles in each group.

4 Six snakes in three groups.

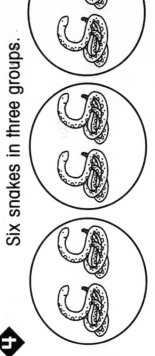

$6 \div 3 =$ _____

There are _____ snakes in each group.

Month-by-Month Math Practice Pages Scholastic Teaching Resources

Answer Key

SEPTEMBER
Counting Apple Seeds, p. 11
Across
b. five
c. two
d. one
e. six
f. nine
h. eight

Down
a. zero
b. four
c. ten
e. seven
g. three

Back-to-School Patterns, p. 12
1. A B
2. A B
3. B C
4. AB
5. ABB
6. ABC
7. Answers will vary.

Picking Apples, p. 13
1. 7 + 1 = 8
2. 5 + 2 = 7
3. 3 + 4 = 7
4. 5 + 0 = 5
5. 6 + 3 = 9
6. 5 + 5 = 10

Garden Shop, p. 14
1. 3
2. 2
3. 5
4. 1
5. 5 – 2 = 3
6. 3 – 1 = 2
7. 4 – 3 = 1

Count the Crop!, p. 15
1. 2
2. 3
3. 2
4. 2
5. Children should color the orange blue.

Apple Snacks, p. 16
1. 2, 3, 1
2. 3, 1, 2
3. 2, 1, 3
4. Children should circle the tree on the right.
5. Children should circle the earmuffs.

A Day With Apples, p. 17
1. 3:00   **5.** 5:00
2. 8:00   **6.** 2:00
3. 11:00   **7.** 9:00
4. 4:00   **8.** 12:00

Apple Pie Pictures, p. 18
1. A   **5.** B
2. B   **6.** A
3. B   **7.** C
4. A

OCTOBER
Create a Jack-o'-Lantern!, p. 19
Answers will vary.

On Halloween Night, p. 20
1. Minute hand on 6; hour hand between 6 and 7
2. Minute hand on 6; hour hand between 6 and 7
3. Minute hand on 6; hour hand between 5 and 6
4. Minute hand on 12; hour hand on 8
5. Minute hand on 12; hour hand on 5
6. Minute hand on 6; hour hand between 7 and 8

Scarecrow Numbers, p. 21

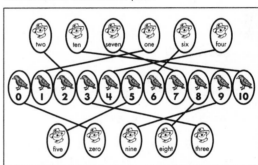

(Not So) Scary Characters!, p. 22
1. 10 cm tall
2. 5 cm tall
3. 9 cm tall

Spooky Symmetry, p. 23
1. yes
2. yes
3. no
4. no
5. Children should draw a horizontal line through the middle of the shape.
6. Children should draw a horizontal or vertical line through the middle of the shape.
7. Children should draw a vertical line through the middle of the shape.

What's in the Tree?, p. 24
1. 8, 2, 6
2. Children should circle the bat.
3. 16

All in a Row, p. 25
1. mouse   **4.** bird
2. bird   **5.** opossum
3. raccoon

Tasty Treats, p. 26
1. 2, 5 Children should circle 5.
2. 4, 3 Children should circle 4.
3. 6, 8 Children should circle 8.
4. 1, 7 Children should circle 7.
5. 8, 0 Children should circle 8.
6. 5, 9 Children should circle 9.

NOVEMBER
Find the Snack!, p. 27
1. B 4   **4.** E 3
2. D 5   **5.** C 6
3. F 1   **6.** A 2

Farm Clues, p. 28
1. Children should circle the 3rd turkey.
2. Children should draw a triangle above the 1st lamb.
3. Children should draw a line under the 1st turkey.
4. Children should draw a square around the 1st scarecrow.
5. Answers will vary.

Turkey Tally, p. 29
Answers will vary.

November Numbers, p. 30
Turkeys run until dinner is done!

It Happens in November, p. 31
1. Children should draw a turkey on the 4th Thursday.
2. Children should draw a red check on the 1st Tuesday.
3. Children should draw a flag on November 11th.
4. Children should color the Saturdays and Sundays green.
5. November 25.

Color the Cornucopia!, p. 32
Children should color the two squares red.
Children should color the two circles orange.
Children should color the three triangles yellow.
Children should color the two rectangles green.
Children should color the two diamonds blue.
Children should color the two pentagons purple.
1. triangle
2. pentagon

Let's Get Cooking!, p. 33
1. 5
2. 4
3. 3
4. 5
5. 2

After the Harvest, p. 34
1. 5, 10, 15, 20, 25, 30
Sentences will vary.
2. 25, 35, 45, 55
3. 15, 20, 30, 35, 50

DECEMBER
Candles and Coins, p. 35
1. 21¢   **3.** 20¢
2. 13¢   **4.** 27¢

The Colors of Kwanzaa, p. 36
A = 5
D = 2
E = 9
G = 3
L = 6
N = 1
K = 8
R = 4
C = 7
B = 0
red, green, and black

Decorations Everywhere!, p. 37
1. Students should circle the snowflake.
2. Students should circle the star.
3. 21

Help the Reindeer!, p. 38

11	20	25	80	85	90	81	32	17	78
9	15	33	47	40	62	5	23	99	17
5	1	51	41	45	35	82	36	53	93
12	10	54	87	55	50	52	26	46	17	27
15	18	63	66	60	31	98	85	90	95	100
7	10	22	77	65	70	75	80	36

Festive Patterns, p. 39
1. ABC
2. ABB
3. ABCC

Holiday Fractions, p. 40
1. Children should color one section on the star.
2. Children should color one section of the ornament.
3. Children should color one section of the present.
4. 1/2
5. 2/6 or 1/3
6. 1/3

Gift Boxes, p. 41
A = 4   **1.** B
B = 9   **2.** C
C = 12   **3.** D
D = 10   **4.** A

Gingerbread People, p. 42
Children should color two squares in the top row.
Children should color three squares in the middle row.
Children should color seven squares in the bottom row.

1.   **2.**   **3.** 12

JANUARY

Winter Wear, p. 43
Wesley can make 9 outfits. Children should color
the bears in any order, in the following combinations:
red top and green bottom, red top and blue bottom,
red top and purple bottom, orange top and green
bottom, orange top and blue bottom, orange top and
purple bottom, yellow top and green bottom, yellow
top and blue bottom, yellow top and purple bottom.

Making Hundreds, p. 44
1. 100
2. 10
3. 80
4. 30
5. 60
6. 50
7. 40

Cold Weather Animals, p. 45
1. whale
2. walrus, polar bear
3. 3 feet
4. penguin
5. walrus, polar bear, whale

Martin Luther King, Jr., p. 46
1. 15
2. That year the Civil Rights Act was signed
and Martin Luther King, Jr. was awarded
the Nobel Peace Prize.
3. 1963

Name Patterns, p. 47
Answers will vary.

Counting by 10s, p. 48

Snowman Math, p. 49
1. (+) 12, (-) 4
2. (+) 2, (-) 0
3. (+) 13, (-) 3
4. (+) 12, (-) 6
5. (+) 5, (-) 3

Mittens on the Clothesline, p. 50
1. 1, 6, 8
2. 1, 4, 7
3. 12, 25, 52
4. 49, 85, 93
5. 17, 24, 54
6. 171, 341, 617

FEBRUARY

Valentine Cards, p. 51

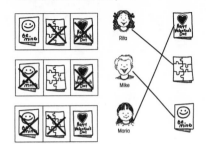

Sweethearts, p. 52
1. 1 tens, 3 ones
2. 2 tens, 1 ones
3. 0 tens, 5 ones
4. 1 tens, 4 ones

Three in a Line, p. 53
Answers will vary.

Fact Families, p. 54
Section 1: Answers will vary.
Section 2:
2, 4, 6, 8, 10, 12, 14, 16, 18, 20
22, 24, 26, 28, 30, 32, 34, 36, 38
40, 42, 44, 46, 48

With Minutes to Go!, p. 55
1. a quarter past
2. half past
3. a quarter 'til
4. half past
5. a quarter past
6. a quarter 'til

Our First President, p. 56
1. 13
2. 5
3. 12
4. 11
5. 4
6. 10
7. 14
8. 9
9. 6
10. 8
11. 7
George Washington

Our 16th President, p. 57

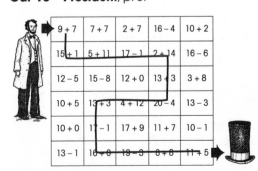

Dental Health Supplies, p. 58
Answers will vary.

MARCH

Lively Leprechauns, p. 59
1. B   4. C
2. A   5. B
3. A

Pots of Gold, p. 60

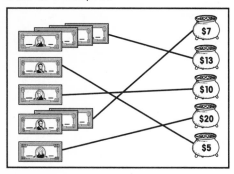

Spot the Pattern!, p. 61
1. Children should circle the second to last boot and draw a clover.
2. Children should circle the clover and draw a horseshoe.
3. Children should circle the hat and draw a clover.
4. Children should circle the boot and draw a hat.

Lucky Fractions, p. 62
1. Children should color in 1 section.
2. Children should color in 3 sections.
3. Children should color in 2 sections.
4. Children should color in 1 whole triangle and 1 section of the other triangle.
5. Children should color in 1 whole square and 1 section of the other square.

Weather Report, p. 63
1. Children should draw a rain cloud on Monday the 21st.
2. Children should draw a snowflake on Saturday the 26th.
3. Children should draw clouds on all days between the 6th and the 12th.
4. Children should draw a sun on Tuesday the 1st.
5. Children should draw a rain cloud on Thursday the 31st.

Colorful Kites, p. 64
In order from left to right:
1. 14, 10, 11
2. 9, 12
3. 13, 8, 14, 11

Flower Petals, p. 65
Children should color 1, 5, 13, 9, 11, 15, 17, 23, and 19 red.
Children should color 2, 4, 6, 8, 10, 14, 18, 20, and 22 yellow.

Spring Happenings, p. 66
1. 2, 1, 3   3. 2, 3, 1
2. 3, 2, 1   4. Children should circle the kite.

APRIL

Fishing Season, p. 67
1. 8 + 7, 6 + 9, 16 - 1
2. 18 - 0, 9 + 9, 5 + 13
3. 11 + 6, 9 + 8
4. 19 - 7, 6 + 6
5. 7 + 7, 19 - 5
6. 8 + 8, 18 - 2, 3 + 13, 19 - 3
7. 5 + 8, 12 + 1
8. 17 - 6

Bunny Math, p. 68
1. 10   6. 10
2. 12   7. 12
3. 12   8. 11
4. 11   9. 12
5. 12   10. 11

The Egg Mystery, p. 69
1. B
2. A
3. D
4. C

Mopsy's Garden, p. 70

More Than a Dozen, p. 71
1. 3
2. 2
3. 2
4. 2
5. Children should color the chick orange.

Let's Recycle!, p. 72
1. plastic jugs
2. newspapers
3. aluminum cans

Will It Happen Today?, p. 73
Answers will vary.

Give Me Five!, p. 74
1. 10, 15, 25, 30, 40, 45, 50, 55
2. 10, 15, 20, 25, 30, 35, 40, 45, 50, 55

MAY

Making Bouquets, p. 75
1. 3 **3.** 5
2. 2 **4.** 12 ÷ 3 = 4

It's Spring!, p. 76
I = 14
Y = 4
A = 9
W = 7
O = 20
H = 6
E = 18
B = 3
N = 10
G = 13
P = 17
F = 11
M = 16
R = 8
L = 15
S = 12
April showers bring May flowers.

Green Thumbs, p. 77

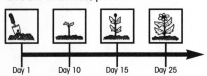

May 2, May 11, May 16, May 26
1. Tuesday
2. Tuesday
3. Friday

Sport Shop, p. 78
25¢, 75¢, $1.25, 50¢, $1.00
1. 50¢
2. 25¢
3. a basketball
4. no

Memorial Day Parade, p. 79

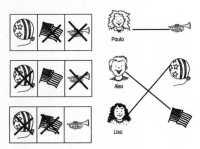

In the Neighborhood, p. 80
1. pet shop
2. library
3. Omar's house
4. baseball diamond

Flower Care, p. 81
1. Minute hand on 6; hour hand between 6 and 7
2. Minute hand on 9; hour hand between 10 and 11
3. Minute hand on 9; hour hand between 3 and 4
4. Minute hand on 9; hour hand on 9

Plenty of Plants, p. 82
1. 1 + 1 = 2, 1 x 2 = 2
2. 2 + 2 + 2 = 6, 2 x 3 = 6
3. 3 + 3 = 6, 3 x 2 = 6

JUNE

Tie Patterns, p. 83
1. ABB **4.** AB
2. ABC **5.** ABB
3. AAB **6.** Answers will vary.

Nick's Busy June, p. 84
1. Saturday
2. Friday
3. June 14th
4. 4
5. Tuesday

Safe and Sound, p. 85
1. bicycle helmets
2. bicycle helmets
3. Answers will vary.

Warm-Weather Weights, p. 86
1. Children should circle the house.
2. Children should circle the baseball.
3. Children should circle the tent.
4. Children should circle the kite.
5. 3, 1, 2
6. 1, 3, 2
7. Answers will vary.
8. Answers will vary.

How Tall?, p. 87
1. Children should circle the tree.
2. Children should circle the balloon.
3. Children should circle the giraffe.
4. 3, 1, 2
5. 2, 1, 3
6. Answers will vary.
7. Answers will vary.

Snack Time, p. 88
1. 3, 2, 1 **3.** 1, 2, 3
2. 1, 2, 3 **4.** 1, 3, 2

Multiplication Riddles, p. 89
1. 4 x 3 = 12 **3.** 2 x 4 = 8
2. 8 x 2 = 16 **4.** 1 x 5 = 5

Riverbank Division, p. 90
1. 4
2. 1
3. 5
4. 2

Notes